Published by Barbour Books, an imprint of Barbour Publishing, Inc., P.O. Box 719, Uhrichsville, Ohio 44683, www.barbourbooks.com

 Member of the
Evangelical Christian
Publishers Association

Printed in China.
5 4 3 2 1

JESUS

Is the Reason for the Season

ELLYN SANNA

Jesus Is the Reason for the Season

In all the rush and bustle of Christmas,
we too often forget
the reason for this season.
There would be no shopping days,
no bright lights on houses and streets,
no Christmas cookies,
or piles of gifts,
if Jesus had not been born.

He was named Jesus,
the name given to him by the angel
even before he was conceived.

LUKE 2:21

Contents

1

A Lonely World

We Need Jesus

We think of Christmas as a time of joy. . .and yet counselors and psychologists know that more people are depressed at Christmas than at any other time of the year. Perhaps Christmas makes us sad because we can't avoid facing the painful difference between what *might* be and what *is,* between the joyful message of Christmas and the reality of our lives.

Christmas insists that life is warm and filled with love—but our own lives may seem empty and cold. Everywhere we turn, we are bombarded with light and song—but the lights may look garish and the music sound tinny if our hearts are full of loneliness.

If we leave Jesus out of Christmas, then this holiday only mocks the earth's pain. But brightly wrapped gifts and cheerful music are not the reasons for Christmas, nor are Christmas trees or frosted cookies or holiday dinners.

Jesus is the only reason for Christmas. His love is the true source of Christmas's joy—and He is present even if we are too depressed to hum a single carol.

Lo, in the silent night
A child to God is born
And all is brought again
That ere was lost or lorn.

Could but thy soul, O man,
Become a silent night!
God would be born in thee,
And set all things a right.

15TH CENTURY

Blessed be the Newborn
who made humanity young again.
Blessed be the Fruit who bowed Himself down for our hunger.
Blessed be the Gracious One who suddenly enriched
all our poverty and filled our need.
Blessed is He whose mercy inclined Him to heal our sickness.

EPHRAEM THE SYRIAN

Our hearts are restless, Lord,
until they find their rest in you.

ST. AUGUSTINE

I sing the birth was born tonight,
the Author both of life and light;
the angels so did sound it.
And like the ravished shepherds said,
who saw the light and were afraid,
yet searched, and true they found it.

BEN JONSON

Jesus Is the Reason for the Season

God, I am lonely for You.
I come to You seeking
the shepherd's eagerness,
the Wise Men's perseverance,
Joseph's trust,
and Mary's obedient heart.
I believe Your Son is the answer to
my loneliness,
my brokenness,
my restlessness,
and my emptiness.
Open my lonely heart to all that Christmas offers.

2

Advent

The Coming of Jesus

Advent is the Latin word that means "the coming" or "to come." It is that space when Christmas has not yet arrived, a time of preparation for the holy moment when the Christ Child breaks through into our lives.

Preparation. . .a time to evaluate life, a time to pray, a time to watch and listen. During Advent we make our hearts ready for Christ by examining how we are living our lives. Is there space for the Holy Child in our busy schedules? Will He be pleased by our thought habits? How can we draw closer to Him? What gifts can we give Him?

Advent reminds us that we should live our lives expectantly, looking for Christ's arrival in our lives, listening for His quiet voice. This is a time for growth and renewal. . .a time to seek Jesus.

*"If you look for me in earnest,
you will find me when you seek me.
I will be found by you," says the LORD.*

JEREMIAH 29:13–14

Seek first his kingdom
and his righteousness.

MATTHEW 6:33 NIV

Advent is filled with busyness,
shopping, planning, baking,
hosting meals, and attending
Christmas parties.
How can we focus on Jesus
when our lives are so hectic,
crammed full with Christmas activities?

We need at least one moment in our day
when we spend some time alone with
the Guest of honor at every Christmas party.
We must stop (if only for a moment),
be quiet,
and seek Jesus.

Be still,
and know that I am God.

PSALM 46:10 NIV

Messenger of good news,
shout to Zion from the mountaintops!
Shout louder to Jerusalem—do not be afraid.
Tell the towns of Judah, "Your God is coming!"
Yes, the Sovereign LORD is coming in all his glorious power.
He will rule with awesome strength.
See, he brings his reward with him as he comes.
He will feed his flock like a shepherd.
He will carry the lambs in his arms,
holding them close to his heart.
He will gently lead the mother sheep with their young.

ISAIAH 40:9–11

Jesus Is the Reason for the Season

Jesus is coming! That is the message Christmas brings.
    Sometimes we misunderstand the message, though. We think
instead that Christmas means we have to be busy. . .
        we have to plan and host and attend countless get-
        togethers with friends and family. . .
            we have to shop and bake and decorate until we
            are exhausted.
And all the while, the Christmas song keeps singing. . .
            offering closeness with God. . .
                His gentle love and care. . .
                His Son.

God may seem far away.
He may not seem to care about the reality of your life.
You may think He does not hear your prayers
or care about your worries.
But He does.
He sent Jesus to tell you that He loves you.
The Creator of the universe
is concerned with the details of your life.
He longs to give you strength
and hope.
He longs to give you Jesus.

O Israel, *how can you say the LORD does not see your troubles?*
How can you say God refuses to hear your case?
Have you never heard or understood?
Don't you know that the LORD is the everlasting God,
the Creator of all the earth?
He never grows faint or weary.
No one can measure the depths of his understanding.
He gives power to those who are tired and worn out;
he offers strength to the weak.
Even youths will become exhausted, and young men will give up.
But those who wait on the LORD will find new strength.
They will fly high on wings like eagles.
They will run and not grow weary.
They will walk and not faint.

ISAIAH 40:27–31

An Advent Tradition

On the morning after Thanksgiving, I reach up into my china cupboard to take down two precious cups and saucers, one for myself and one for my husband. Each morning throughout Advent we sip our coffee from these Christmas cups.

When I fill my cup with rich brown liquid, it warms my hands, then fills my mouth, and readies me for my day. And as I sip, I fill my mind with thoughts of Jesus. For me, my coffee cup is a symbol of Advent's spiritual preparation, a small yearly ritual that reminds me to ready my home, my life, and my heart for Christ's coming.

Throughout the days of Advent, I welcome family and friends into my home. Together we celebrate Jesus' coming to earth so long ago. And through all the bright, busy days, my Christmas coffee cup reminds me to keep my focus on Jesus, the reason for this happy season.

How will you welcome Jesus this Advent season? What simple traditions will remind you to prepare your life and heart for Him?

_____

_____

_____

_____

_____

_____

_____

_____

_____

_____

_____

Take time to pray. . .
it helps bring God near
and washes the dust of earth
from your eyes.
Take time for friends. . .
they are the source of happiness.
Take time for work. . .
it is the pride of success.
Take time to think. . .
it is the source of power.
Take time to read. . .
it is the foundation of knowledge.

Take time to laugh. . .
it is the singing that
helps with life's loads.
Take time to love. . .
it is the one sacrament of life.
Take time to dream. . .
it hitches the soul to the stars.
Take time to play. . .
it is the secret of youth.
Take time to worship. . .
it is the highway to reverence.

ANONYMOUS

During this time of Advent,
may you take time for the important things in life—
the things that give your life meaning
and bring you joy.
And most of all,
may you take time for Jesus,
the reason for this season.

3

Christmas

The Birthday of God's Son

Jesus Is the Reason for the Season

In every heart lies a Bethlehem.
A place where light shines with tender memories.
A place where the song of angels still echoes.
A place of wonder, awe, and peace.
In this place, the humility of shepherds,
the wisdom of the Magi, and
the dreams of a mother and father all meet.
Most of all, Bethlehem moments are filled,
and overflowing,
with the presence of Jesus.

Treasure your Bethlehems,
those quiet moments when Jesus
is born into your life.

Jesus Is the Reason for the Season

What are the Bethlehem moments that you have experienced (this year and in the past)?

_____

_____

_____

_____

_____

_____

_____

_____

_____

_____

_____

Jesus Is the Reason for the Season

The Son of God, the eternal King,
that did us all salvation bring,
and freed the soul from danger;
He whom the whole world could not take,
the Word, which heaven and earth did make,
was now laid in a manger.

BEN JONSON

How can you create a spiritual manger in your heart, a place where the Christ Child will rest?

_____

_____

_____

_____

_____

_____

Jesus Is the Reason for the Season

Sometimes Christmas goes by in a blur of laughter, food, and wrapping paper. In all the busyness, we may miss the very reason for our celebration—Jesus. We need to set aside a quiet moment to celebrate His birthday.

Here are some ideas:

- Light a candle and read Psalm 61, making the words your prayer.
- Sit by the Christmas tree and read Luke 2:1–20.
- Write a letter to God.
- List the blessings in your life.
- While you listen to Christmas music, examine your life and look for ways you could be closer to Jesus.

Jesus Is the Reason for the Season

Christmas day declares that he dwelt among us. . . . This is the festival which makes us know, indeed, that we are members of one body; it binds together the life of Christ on earth with his life in heaven; it assures us that Christmas day belongs not to time but to eternity.

FREDERICK DENISON MAURICE

The ox and the ass understood more of the first Christmas than the high priests in Jerusalem. And it is the same today.

THOMAS MERTON

On Christmas Day,
may you experience
moments of eternity,
and may you feel
the humble presence
of Jesus.

4

Emmanuel

God with Us—Forever

Jesus Is the Reason for the Season

The Christmas message from God is one of great joy.
    Yet when the angels brought the news to
        Mary,
            Joseph,
                and the shepherds,
                    they were all afraid.
To each of them, the angels' parting words were,
    "Do not be afraid.
        God is with you."
That is God's message to you today:
    "Don't be afraid.
        I am with you always."

And be sure of this:
I am with you always.

MATTHEW 28:20

YOU *need not be afraid. . .*
for the LORD *is your security.*

PROVERBS 3:25–26

Jesus Is the Reason for the Season

Christmas is a time to believe.
  I believe that:

_____

_____

_____

_____

Christmas is a time to rejoice.
  I will rejoice in:

_____

_____

_____

_____

Christmas is a time to love.
  I will share my love by:

_____

_____

_____

_____

Jesus Is the Reason for the Season

Christmas is time to seek Jesus.
  I will seek Him by:

_____

_____

_____

_____

Christmas is a time to offer thanks.
  I will say "thank you" by:

_____

_____

_____

_____

Christmas is a time to recognize Jesus' constant presence in my life.
  I see Jesus in these places:

_____

_____

_____

_____

There is inescapable logic in the
Christmas message:
we experience joy,
quite simply, in self-surrender,
in giving up our lives.
Joy calls for renunciation.

LADISLAUS BOROS

Give yourself away at Christmas—
and all year long.
When you do, you will find you are not diminished.
Instead, you will feel the presence of
Jesus' joy inside your heart.

Creating God,
who made the moon and stars to light the night
and the sun to light the day;
we bless and thank You for Christ,
Light of the world.
He is a lamp unto our feet
and a light unto our path.
He is our way, our truth, and our life.
Amen.

ANONYMOUS

Optimism,
a "taste for happiness,"
is a basic and essential aspect of
being a Christian.

LADISLAUS BOROS

At Christmas, and all through the year,
may you experience the "taste for happiness"
that only Jesus gives.
May you know He is always with you.